ALIVE IN THIS PLACE

Susan Dworski Nusbaum

Kenmore, WA

Epicenter Press
6524 NE 181st St.
Suite 2
Kenmore, WA 98028
www. Epicenterpress.com
www. Coffeetownpress.com
www. Camelpress.com

For further information go to www.coffeetownpress.com or www.susandworskinusbaum.com

All rights reserved. No part of this book may be reproduced or transmitted in any form or by any means, electronic or mechanical, including photocopying, recording, or any information storage and retrieval system, without permission in writing from the publisher.

This is a work of fiction. Names, characters, places, brands, media, and incidents are the product of the author's imagination or are used fictitiously.

Cover designer: Dawn Anderson
The cover image: Mixed media photograph, "Elemental Forest," by Mary Jane Nusbaum

Alive in this Place
2019 © Susan Dworski Nusbaum

ISBN: 9781603815475 (trade paper)
ISBN: 9781603815604 (ebook)

Printed in the United States of America

For Ruth, my mother

I am grateful for the encouragement and
mentorship of Philip Terman, Ansie Baird, and the
Chautauqua writers' community and as always, for
the love, support, and inspiration of my children,
grandchildren, sister, and friends.

Acknowledgements

These poems have appeared or will appear in the following publications:

Home: Buffalo Spree Magazine; The Buffalo News

The Comfort of Summer Trees: The Woven Tale Press

Mockingbird: The Woven Tale Press

July Poems: Calliope (June, 2020)

The Way In: The Buffalo News

Coming of Age: The Buffalo News

Like Ordinary Weeping: The Buffalo News

Table of Contents

Acknowledgements

I...above the canopy

Paradise 3
The Comfort of Summer Trees 5
Home 7
The Way In 9
Eavesdrop 11
Not with Ghostly Voices 13
Real Estate 15
The Closing 17
The Ordinary 19
I Am Afraid of This Rain 21
Ephemera 23
This Snow 25
Afterloss 27
Alive in This Place 29

II...never lost, never lost

Earth Shine 33
Phone Calls 35
Recipe File 37
Ruth 39
Footprints 41
Butterfly 43
Hikkaduwa Beach 45
July Poems 47
Beach Rose 51
To Husband is a Verb 53

Patience 55
Piece by Piece 57
More of the Same 59
Spilt Milk 61
Regret 63

III...like ordinary weeping
Gloves 67
Like Ordinary Weeping 69
Girl Waiting: Nepal 71
Hanoi 73
Sightseeing in Ronda 75
Jun Yan 77
Inside Story 79
About Perfection 81
Affliction 83
Armed & Dangerous 85
The Hat 87
Nelson Mandela Tells a Story 89
Gluttony 91

IV...scouting the distance
Anthem 95
Mockingbird 97
Returning 99
Scouting the Distance 101
Apollo at Fifteen 103
American Girls 105
Coming of Age 107
November 109
Changes 111

Genesis	113
The Bathing Suit	115
In Praise of Geometry	117
Honeycrisp	119
Flag	121
We Never Close	123

I.
...above the canopy

Paradise

Don't tell anyone,
but this is heaven— right here.
Yes, that deafening rap music,
horns honking under a granite sky,
the frigid wind shivering outside the door,
melting polar cap, scourge of wildfires,
villages and coastlines vanishing.

And what, you may ask,
of a welcoming shore for the tired, the poor?
What of the Jerusalem sung on Sundays?
Land of the free? Justice for all?
Get your head out of the clouds.

This is all we've got—
a dollar, warm from holding,
slipped into a homeless hand,
the touch of a chemo-nurse
swabbing a pale arm,
a grandchild's distant voice,
phone call from a forgotten friend.

And yes, we can count on
those fiery daylilies opening at dawn,
and Canada geese in their iridescent finery
returning in April. Miraculously,
tiny chartreuse leaves

will unfurl each spring
over the ashy limbs of winter elms,
and the sun's light will bounce
off the face of each new moon.
You can depend on it.

So, this is the Kingdom of Heaven,
where god lives.
Eight hours of daylight,
sixteen dark ones.

The Comfort of Summer Trees

Summer trees lead separate lives from winter trees.
There's no ceremony, no parade to mark their arrival.

After the winter ghosts, frost-sheared elms
have been exorcised, and the frozen silence,

floes of grieving have melted,
a lush canopy appears in full leaf,

limbs drape their heavy foliage
over streets crisscrossing old neighborhoods,

alive with the singing of phoebes and locusts,
the commotion of termites, the air

perfumed with cut grass mingled with mold.
All is softness now,

even the bark-skin beneath your fingers,
and loopy roots shining like snakes among myrtle.

Suddenly— a city of solace, its passageways
lined with the generosity of maples

and arching birches, whose tiny leaves
shiver like confetti against the summer sky.

Home

I've had many, but this one,
this cozy aerie on the 7th floor, is the last.

I've traded the grateful garden, the fish pond,
extra space for children and guests,

for the arches and high ceilings of another era,
sturdy doors, thick concrete walls,

perfect for hanging photos of foreign travels
and the all-too-vivid dead.

But the best part is the vista.
I can see across broad expanses,

swaths of paintbrush treetops,
birds looping, swirling in the ecstasy of freedom,

peaked red roofs sending up wisps
of chimney smoke over the familiar

rivers and bridges, distant steeples I can name,
the mist of Niagara Falls visible in April.

My windows open wide into a world
above the canopy which once limited my vision.

At last I can see across lifetimes—dappled morning
melting into a white-feathered sky,

the mysterious gathering
of thunderheads at the horizon,

a satiny darkness sweeping-in, opaque
but shimmering with reflected light.

The Way In

Too cold to go outside.
Through the frozen window
I project myself to the sidewalk,
inhale the smell of chimney smoke,
moldering leaves, wet wool,

imagine myself trudging down Lafayette
breathing hard, sliding over icy paths
past lumpy lawns white as sky,
arriving at the busy co-op among
down-wrapped, patchy-faced shoppers,

collective brows furrowed in concentration—
which organic pear? which onion?—
staying inside the shared warmth,
the easy conversation, longer than necessary,
waiting for the sun to arc a little higher

before I stride through the automatic doors,
retrace my steps, never mind the cold
seeping into my boots, searing my throat,
sing to myself one or two verses
of You Are My Sunshine until

I see my home rising up at the corner,
a new clarity propelling me forward,
showing me the way in.

Eavesdrop

Step into the corner under the eaves
where ice destroyed the gutter last winter,

and rainwater gushes into the garden,
the *eavesdrop*, a space just outside of inside.

You'll find yourself
behind a curtain glittering darkly

listening to your heartbeat,
face drenched but tilted upward

to overhear your heart's whispered secrets
mingled with the sounds of your own breathing,

secrets bubbling into the cup of your ear,
the way you might decipher

the gossip of starlings
or bees' murmured conversations,

clear as wind-chimes
glissando-ing through the spray.

Not with Ghostly Voices

An overnight snow quilts the skylight,
curves around door jambs and ledges,
mute insulation against a shovel's thin scrape,
tin whistle of ambulance, vibrations
releasing attic noises through the ceiling,

where love letters in fat sheaves
pop hinges on valises, dislodge
trophies clattering from the shelf,
boxes shift with the bulk of inherited china,
silver platters tarnished with disuse,

where leather diaries exhale
the cold breath of secrets,
loose photos flutter under eaves like spinnakers,
where a cradle sings a lullaby
on its broken spindle—*hush, little baby*—
and stuck in a crack between rafters,
a poem weeps,

as a chorus swells,
not with ghostly voices,
or, god forbid, the rustle of mice,
but the sounds of decades
adrift through the floor-boards—
a rich polyphony, this chill morning—
then dissolving mid-air
in a flash of sun on glass,
and a snowplow's thunderous applause.

Real Estate

I have lived hap-
hazardly in this house
for 25 years, with faded
yellow tulips on the table,
tax documents and travel slides
cluttering the attic,
bricks of brown sugar
sharing cupboard space
with outdated tomato paste,
a jumble of wire hangers
and uncomfortable shoes
inhabiting my closet floor.

Soon I will scoop up the debris,
toss it into the dumpster,
and pay off the mortgage.
The important things—a red blanket,
some books, my piano—
I will carry on the shell on my back
like a crab, sidle out the door,
find a simpler habitat to contain me,
unencumbered by remorse or greed,
my debts forgiven, a niche
more suitable for my needs,

where I will molt
my creviced, horny skin
and grow a smooth one,
tender and translucent.
No need for a ctr ent,
WBF or att gar.
No need for ottomans or clocks
or Persian rugs.
I'll be tidier, more secure,
the master,
not the trespasser.
And the place will embrace me
gratefully.

The Closing

All night I listened to the trees,
bouquets of russet groaning
under the burden of snow,
as branches creaked and cracked,
surrendered to porches built long ago
with jogs to accommodate them,
wedding canopies bending
to unbearable weight, clefts—
perfect rungs for boosting small soles—
now sheared from their ladders,
blank spaces left where sparrows
marshaled the seasons
and squirrels rooted for sustenance.

This morning the next owner
surveys the chaos in the garden,
the birch he prized, the sale-clincher,
split by the freak October snowfall,
paper skin peeled back, gold coins
strewn spendthrift across the lawn.
He climbs over the sycamore,
which weeks before had enticed him
with its mottled bark and broad shade,
bows his head before nests of weeping-
cherry boughs, next spring's pink cascades
crushed to pulp against the stone wall.

I open the window to him.
Can I abandon this framed landscape,
my diary, my solace?
Through the scrolling snow,
eddies of departure swirl
like phantom arms from bared trunks.
Disorder defines our grieving,
his for the losing, mine for the leaving.

The Ordinary

Daily morning coffee—
when shards of night-dreams
vanish in curls of steam,
and thin yellow slices slide
through window panes
along formica countertops
and up the doorframe,
rimming the wall-clock's face
with a fiery ring.

Let the ritual begin!

Bach on the radio,
eyes closed, lips on the lip
of this hallowed mug—
a cavernous chip
gouged into its bottom—
poised to tip wherever it rests,
wobbles and sloshes,
teeters with tidal waves
of French Roast.

Pour carefully.
Hold the cup gently to avoid
spillage, jagged edges,
blood on the napkin.
Drink quickly, never mind
the burn on the tongue, in the throat.
Refuse to set it down
until the waking is over,
and every bitter drop is gone.

I Am Afraid of This Rain

Not a merciful,
not a nourishing rain;
the kind that seeps through
invisible cracks in basements,
smells of mold and rabbit urine.
This rain drives slant through eaves,
through skylights and the panes
of summer rooms,
the kind that turns
children limp, lovers sour.
This rain invades the marrow,
like news of a spreading cancer
or an uncontainable oil spill.
Fists of clouds pummel the sky.
I can cover my ears against
the shudder, the sigh,
but this rain slaps me,
spins me—and, ah!
there you are, silhouetted
in the porch doorway—
you in your red slicker,
lifting a fallen begonia,
setting it upright on the step.

Ephemera

A darkening sky,
split by thunder. Rain
obliterates the elms,
embroiders willow-
patterns on the glass,
panes embossed
with scattered splats
of graffiti, each liquid
abstraction vanishing
the instant it appears,
temporal pleasures
sliding down, forming,
washing away,
changing like the
faces of children,
lost before the brain
can fully absorb
their splendor,
features preserved
in the mind's eye
to dissolve into new ones,
beheld and held
for only an instant,
    this passing montage
        accompanied by jazz improvisation—
           syncopations on the sill,
               walking-bass against an awning,
                   a blue wind wailing at the window.

This Snow

What I thought was ash
is a certain kind of snow,
a silent grey particulate
filming over roofs and driveways,
dampness in the air
dissipating the flamboyant sunrise
that just minutes ago
blazed from the horizon.

What saddens me isn't the gloom
but the suddenness of the shift
from glorious to ominous,
shocking but not arbitrary,
forces real and explainable
over which I have no control.

I think of other Januarys,
of quilted lawns and softened branches,
the silence broken only
by the chatter of sparrows in the hedge,
the squeals of children making angels.
This snow smolders with a pervasive absence,
as I feel the earth turning,
and wait for another burning sunrise.

Afterloss

May appears with scars again this year.
Lightning struck to ash the limbs

of overhanging elms along the road to Mayville,
leaving keloids the size of Lake Chautauqua

weeping in their gray bark.
But from the gash where shade had been,

light pours blue to gold, igniting
dust of mustard weed on greening pastures.

Around the curve, the weathered barn,
collapsed at last from winter's weight,

leaves the landscape rearranged,
its remnants picked by mice or sold for scrap,

and in exchange, the earth lies steaming,
new-plowed furrows streaked with silver.

Like a scrawny crow jabbing last year's apple,
grief pecks at my shriveled heart,

yet dazzled by a lightening sky,
I take the steps two at a time to my front door,

where brazen azaleas poke through the porch rails,
blazing all shades for my return.

Alive in This Place

Now that I'm rooted at last
inside a space where I think I belong,

why do I still dream of other settings—
pine-paneled rooms with views of dunes
and osprey nests on telephone poles,
salt air breathing through louvered shutters?

Yet here I am, alive in this place,
soothed by traffic sounds whooshing by,
where I linger every night
in the old paisley wing chair
watching amber panes of street-light
spill silently across my Turkish carpet,
slide over the Tuscan landscape
above the mantle.

And there he is, Sandy,
smiling from his frame,
keeping me company. Sandy,
slouched in his Eames chair,
swirling a purple Bordeaux
in a long-stemmed crystal goblet,
savoring the departing light.

II
...never lost, never lost

Earth Shine

In the cradle of the newborn crescent,
a weathered face, familiar as my own,
etched in solar light from earth's day-side,
a wisp of distant incandescence, dawn
rekindled on the darkened round of moon.
Its glow illuminates this shadowed camp,
with flickerings of daylight strewn across
the lunar face, tossed back again and sifted
through the starry haze. And as I drift
into uneasy dreams, I re-collect
my yesterdays, never lost, never lost,
gliding back to earth like an autumn leaf,
paler now, remote, but pulsing life.

Phone Calls
for Patty

Now we speak on the phone
of ailments, the heartbreak of losing people.
Under each conversation we imagine ourselves,
sisters eight years apart holding hands,
hear the faint chatter—the hum
of hopscotch, piano recitals,
reading "Our Town" aloud on the porch glider.

Long distance, we remember each other
in Peter Pan collars and penny loafers,
crying over romances gone bad,
disappointments, the hurdles of parenthood.
Age makes no difference now.

Squeezed into the inescapable present,
we're united by inevitable decline,
sharing boredom and loneliness and arthritis,
and a new closeness, a tenderness
children rarely feel for each other,
enhanced by the sounds of years long gone,
the urgency of the few remaining.

Recipe File

In a script shrunk by Parkinson's,
she lists the ingredients from memory—
walnuts, finely chopped,

dates snipped with kitchen scissors,
sweet butter, creamed by hand
with eggs, sugar, one cup, scant.

Year after year, my mother sets out
the flowered china for Rosh Hashanah,
late roses and hydrangea in a crystal bowl,

polished silver candlesticks, flames flickering
each time the door opens, smoky autumn chill
mingled with the scent of onions,

perfumed aunts in open-toed shoes, fox stoles,
and uncles, heavy in overcoats, coughing,
stinking of Camels.

She wipes her cherry fingertips on her apron,
ladles into blue-veined Meissen bowls
yellow chicken broth, rich with secrets—

celery tops, parsnips, a sprig of dill,
next, beef brisket slow-simmered on a bed of onions,
potatoes roasted until their skins crackle,

a hint of bay and cinnamon,
passed down from a mysterious ancestor,
Moroccan, perhaps, or Persian.

After enough time has passed,
and every speck of *fleisch* is cleared,
she brushes crumbs into her open palm,

passes a clean napkin to each person
for the final offering—torte layers,
dark and moist, a crown of cream.

With a grand gesture,
my mother cuts the first slice,
her hand steady, no trace of tremor.

Ruth

Two sisters caught in a thunderstorm,
we stumble over grassy mounds
holding each other up,
past the Temple Beth El dead—
Lapides, Cohen, Amdursky—
resting where you might have been.

Drenched, we quit our search,
go for a quiet lunch, the window view
obscured by a curtain of rain,
reflect on how you concealed
the emotions we share as aging widows,
admitting we may have been unreceptive
to your despair—our father's death,
fear of your own, your loneliness,

each of us wanting to please you,
but reluctant to let you into our hectic lives,
courting your attentions but keeping you
outside looking in—an honored guest,
never lifting the veil of privacy
you always wore.

Did we ever know you, Mother?
Over quiche, we find glimpses—
Chanel and Mozart,
tiny hats with veils, white gloves,
manicured fingers turning pages.
Perhaps we were deaf to your telling.
Perhaps you were merciful.

Footprints
An Unidentified Family Portrait c. 1885

Whispering across the photograph,
a haze blurs the edges of everything,
bushes in the foreground by a trampled path,
a ghostly shape at the right corner of the wooden plank
    house,
a horse and cart to the left, where an uncle, perhaps,
sits with a small baby.

No, I can't journey to Poland
to find this family—every trace erased.
But they're here for a moment,
stiff in their best clothes—
mustachioed men, women in long skirts,
children in party finery,
even on this warm summer day.

If I could, I'd trudge up the path, search
their unsmiling faces up-close for clues.
Would I detect a family resemblance?
Great-grandfather Beryl's big ears?
A jowl, a nose, a head full of curls?
That toddler in the center, is he
my grandfather Maurice?

I'd ride with Beryl each day 12 miles
by horse-cart over farmland
from Raczki to Suvalki,
selling dry-goods door to door,

help Miriam hang the wash
from the twisted clothesline
strung across the leafy background.

I'd weep with this couple as they send
their children off one by one at 15,
to America or Palestine or Argentina,
to save them from conscription or Cossacks,
unable to imagine their distant struggles,
or hear the ominous goosesteps
approaching their own.

No, you won't find my footprints
on their front stoop. But theirs are visible
as I stand at that narrow door, pausing
before my own door closes behind me,
holding for an instant a sacred imprint
binding my existence to theirs,
to keep and tuck into my suitcase
when I set off on my next journey.

Butterfly

She never liked opera
until he surprised her one birthday
by taking her to the Met for *Butterfly*,
pretending the seats were in the Family Circle,
but guiding her into the third-row orchestra,
where, already married more than a few years,
she became a young bride again,
as Cio-Cio-San's ardor made the air tremble
with her love for Pinkerton, arousing in her
all the passion a wife can harbor,
unaware of the ship on the horizon
sailing steadily toward the shoals.

Hikkaduwa Beach
Ceylon 1970

Fresh limeade on a white verandah.
   our children laughing in the sand,
      briny sprays spinning off gulls' wings,
         scent of brinjal curry spiraling from the kitchen.

You, curled under a mosquito net,
   both of us sheltered from the restlessness,
      the monotony of home, eddies of resentment.

So young, we are. So confident,
   sharing a year-long adventure
      in an island sanctuary,
         thinking we're invulnerable,

unaware of the revolution fomenting even now
   in the tea-softened mountains of this paradise,
      where we feel solid, coherent,

unprepared for the centrifugal forces poised
   to fling us apart as we swirl across continents,
      returning to the perilous world lying in wait.

July Poems

1. One Afternoon in Late July

Just before the storm,
we sat on the porch in Adirondack chairs,
thighs sticking to the paint,
a film of sweat on every inch of skin.

Silence tumbled through the screen door.
A mask of grey gauze transformed
the sun into moon.

We quarreled, mired in bitterness,
gestured slow-motion through thick air,
voices muffled, as if under water,
waited for thunder to save us.

A dopplering siren, a distant radio.
Schumann's Traumerai
spiraling toward an equivocal sky.

We lowered the awning,
desperate for the ping of revival,
a cleansing downpour, gutter-slosh.

The trees held their breath.

2. One Evening in Late July

A single streak of sun
played over grassy patches
under the sycamore,
dissolved behind the porch.
Children hopscotched, voices lowered,
as day began to pull away.
    Soon, the calling-in.

Through a window, a golden light
moved across the rug and disappeared.
We sank into the couch inside
the intersecting haloes of table lamps,
considered the paths we had taken,
words stumbling slowly into the darkness,
    abandoned summer dreams.

Before climbing the stairs,
you clicked the lights off one by one,
turned to pull a Black-eyed Susan
from a plastic tumbler on the coffee table,

arranged it carefully behind my ear,
kissed my lips.
    Somewhere, music was playing.

3. One Morning in Late July

I remember a silent morning like this one,
when you and I slipped away in the early hours,

all that weeping and shouting finished
months before, wounds healing over.

We untied Calypso and slid off across Lake Ontario,
sails filled just enough to still the flapping,

only the swish of our wake spreading behind us,
the squeak of sheets against winches,

each of us sinking down
into our own thoughts, not speaking.

As the wind shifted, you adjusted some lines,
and when it stopped, we dropped the sail.

The shrouds trembled,
sending vibrations through our bodies,

and there in the deepest part of the lake
we rocked under a sky swept with foam.

Although we could barely see the shoreline,
we knew exactly where we were.

Beach Rose

We loved the wild beach roses
covering the dunes at the Cape,
bright petals, leaves wrinkled like mint
on thorny stems planted in sand,

sweet barrier between us
and the slap of waves at high tide,
but low enough for watching sunsets.

When we left we pulled a few,
stuck them in a plastic bag on the back seat,
laughing at our foolishness—what chance
they'd anchor in our loamy garden,

far from salt air and sandy terrain,
suddenly separated from the terns who rested
inside their foliage, mice at their roots?

We shoved them carelessly into the earth,
hoping they'd accept the transplant,
lend us their resilience,

show us the tenacity we needed inside
the teetering structures of our pale habitat,
the resolve to repair them.

Next spring, shoots rose among the tulips,
spreading across black soil,
poking into rows of onions and asparagus,
the debris of our winter lives lit

by neon signs of spring,
baskets of red hips in autumn,
sour globes ready to make sweet jam,
and tonics for whatever ailed us.

Every morning at sunrise, we could smell
the ocean in the unfolding blossoms,
hear gulls flapping in the distance.

To Husband is a Verb

Even toward the end, you husbanded my hope,
pretending that this unspeakable illness
was a temporary detour, that we'd return
to everyday, we'd laugh and travel, visit the kids, make love.

You suffered my wife-ing, endured therapies
for my peace of mind, drank my chicken soup
when your tongue was numb to taste.

Each night you watered the plants,
set up the morning coffee, added to the grocery list.
You exhaled into my open palm to keep me breathing,
kissed my eyelids while I pretended to sleep.

All this you did to shelter me, as you'd always done,
tenderly husbanding my life's flickering trajectory.

Patience

Sparrows in the hedge on edge,
chirping their heads off in the dark,
anxious as infants waiting for a breast—
don't they know it's 4 AM?

Nervous cicadas staccato
their impatience from every maple.
Even the doves mourn for morning.
They'd drum their fingers if they had any.

You can't jump-start sunrise.
In three more hours the day
will bounce from its murky bed,
and slide open the window.

And the prolonged vigil over a dying husband—
the pacing, the self-reproach,
fingernails bitten to bleeding,
the urgent prayers for an end to suffering,
the wished-for death. Night

will come, I promise,
sure as sunrise.

Piece by Piece

After you died
I could assemble
every hair, every bone,
conjure you up whole
whenever I needed to.
Now twenty years later,
I see you in pieces—
the light hair on your arm,
the way your ears
lay flat to your head,
the nape of your neck.

Leaning at the kitchen counter.
our son tells jokes in your voice
with your dazzling grin,
wave of your hand.
In photos, yes, that's your shoulder,
the tension in your body.
I think I can remember
your eyes squinting,
rogue eyebrows, full lips.

Sometimes I dream
of that time you walked away,
face darkened, blind to me.
I've lost the face you wore
when you returned.

More of the Same

Winter's siege came early this year.
A silent battlefield streams
past this train's window,
branches like broken swords
crisscrossing white pastures,

suspended after-snow,
tufts of ruptured milkweed,
hovering above shattered ponds,
brittle mounds of yellow leaves
frozen in clumps.

The granite air has lost its luster
with the chafe of grit on glass,
as grinding wheels clack-clack me to sleep
through a tunnel, eyes closed against
darkness, black on black.

What will greet this train?
More of the same—scarred landscape,
shrouded sun, bitter wind.
No illusions hover here. Uncoupled,
I'll keep on going, keep on going.

Spilt Milk

I dreamed I poured
an entire quart of milk
meant for your Frosted Flakes
into a wastebasket.
In that dream, we stood
at the kitchen counter,
and looked at each other in shock
for one split second,
and began to laugh so hard
our chests heaved with the effort,
shoulders shaking,
tears sloshing down our faces
into our cereal,
and I experienced
such relief, such energy,
I woke up smiling,
and smiled the rest of the day,
suddenly feeling my lungs inflated,
a sensation I'd been missing
while I held my breath
during the long year of your dying.
No more crying!

Regret

In the Wegman's parking lot, I heard
a little girl calling "Mommy, Mommy,"
as if her mother might drop her groceries
and fly up to catch the yellow balloon
escaped from her hand.

And for one second, I thought
I could jump high enough to grab it,
but, of course I couldn't, that impulse
reflecting my need to put everything right,

so I decided then and there not to regret
anything that should have been, but wasn't,
or was, that shouldn't have been,
the good intentions gone awry,

hours wasted on the impossible,
kind words left unsaid,
bad advice I gave my children,
 ("go to law school," I said, "play the viola,")

my distain for my husband's
experiments in Chinese cooking,
or my condescending manner toward Tracy,
the only African-American girl
in my high school class,

and I say to myself, "Let it go,
you can't undo your mistakes, intentional or not,
and don't expect to be forgiven—
no Yom Kippur litany will make them disappear.

You can't just leap up
to correct things gone bad—
they're done, floating in the sky,
reflected in the upturned faces

of all the people on this earth you've injured,
and those already gone,
who are batting around that balloon
filled with your deficiencies,
and, I hope, having a grand old time.

III
...like ordinary weeping

Gloves

Sirens shriek— police and ambulance,
knot of gawkers, corner Pineapple and Main.
I glimpse the man I've greeted most mornings,
now propped on a metal bench stone-still,
eyes closed, pony-tail loosened over shoulders,
a tattooed heart—GINA— on his bicep.
His shorts droop unzipped beneath a distended
belly, buttocks exposed, almost naked.
The cops circle his body keeping their distance,
pull on plastic gloves in order to move him.
I don't linger to watch, but continue on my way
to Whole Foods. And all afternoon I wonder
if she'll claim him, bathe the stench from his body,
tie up his hair, trace the red tattoo with her bare fingers.

Like Ordinary Weeping
Indian Girl Weeps Stones, Delhi Times

First, the pain pools behind the eyes
like ordinary weeping,
but when the girl Saviti
squeezes her lids together,
not tears, but small white stones
drop with the sound of wind-chimes
into the sling of her sarong.

Squatting in the sun
along the Jarkhand-Airport Road,
Saviti crushes limestone slabs to pebbles
with the rhythmic chink and ping of the pick,
chalk invading her nostrils, shoulders bent
under the thunder of the jet-stream,

the heft of gravel scooped into baskets
and balanced on her head to the weigh-station.
What desiccates your tears, Saviti?
Is it an unrelenting thirst from a life
smothered beneath layers of grit?

Yet every night Saviti trudges to her village
through dark excavations, inhales
the Holy Ganges in the distance,
and raises her eyes to sip nourishment
from a star-shattered sky.

Girl Waiting: Nepal
(a photograph)

Elbow propped behind her on the ledge,
she leans against a pine wall streaked

by monsoon rains blown cold
across the foothills of the Himalayas,

barely hears the stable rustling
beyond the topknot of her hair

or feels the brown sack slung across her body
and skew of her blouse straining

to flower beneath a drape of wool,
doesn't sense the somber sash

drooping loose along the length of thigh,
toes poked pink from sandals in a vee.

Can it be the clip of hooves,
or dusky whistle of a lover,

that tightens her lips, quickens her breath,
turns her cheeks toward paddies cropped from view,

or is it the slipping sun
that pinches the brow between her eyes

searching, searching down the rosy footpath
far beyond the frame?
A bus has come and gone,
diesel clouds obscure the gravel underfoot,

but still she waits suspended in the half-light
for a touch to warm her face, to lift her eyes,

erase the furrows etched between them,
make her lips bloom.

Hanoi

After the French restaurant,
the celestial ile flottante,
we join the stream of bicycle taxis

flowing down Trang Tien Boulevard,
bells swelling the dusk
all the way to the French Opera House,

where inside the great hall,
a Japanese string quartet
plays Brahms and Tchaikovsky

for an audience of foreigners,
as the jangle of bells, smells
of grilled pork, whispers of the war-dead

float through open windows,
reminding us we are castaways
in a sea of strangers.

Sightseeing in Ronda

Every morning the citizens of Ronda
navigate the ancient Roman cobblestones
to cross the 18th century Puente Nuevo,
where 20th century Civil War dissidents
were flung into the ravine to their death.

They press on to the market, cathedral,
past windows bordered blue and mustard,
crumbling Moorish palaces,
past the bull ring, the chocolateria,
McDonalds, the internet café,

nod *buenos dias* as they traverse
black and white tiled patterns in the plaza,
lingering for a while under the poplar trees
outside the Guitar House to hear
Paco Seco play Terrega or Bach,

shake their heads as they watch
gargantuan sightseeing buses snort
through the tangle of narrow *calles*,
ears ringing with the babble of foreigners
jabbing at souvenir mugs in shop windows.

Oh, for the serenity of evening, they sigh,
while they wait patiently on benches
to join the *paseo* through the *alameda*,
gathering for dinner at 10, a comfortable hour,
much too late for tourists.

Jun Yan

She vacuums the runner, scrubs the terrazzo,
polishes the brass in the condo elevator,
face gleaming in burnished panels.

Sweeping gestures shape her story—
one-year email friendship, then marriage,
flight from her Chinese village
to Buffalo for a prosperous life.

In halting English, she explains—
her mother admired her grace at birth,
named her Jun Yan, "beautiful swallow."
With scissor-fingers she mimes
the bird's tail in flight.

Trailing a billow of blue smock,
she swoops and flutters, plucks
clean rags from a nest by the door,
slender arms reaching
to dust the crystal chandelier.

An illumination, prayer in flight.
Elegy for a lost mother.

Inside Story

I dread those Fridays when Wilma comes to clean,
suffering her crazy chatter, busying myself
with tasks in other rooms, as she rails
over the growl of the Hoover
against Walmart and high taxes,
a healthcare system broke beyond repair,
a government plot to poison the air,

scattering curses with her broom,
at repairmen—her leaky roof, caved-in porch,
never done, never done right—
and stupid cops—she knows the characters
in every local rape and murder, offers
undisclosed evidence, her own—the *real* truth.
They don't have a clue, she says.
After she's gone, I find her
misspelled notes in shaky writing,
instructions on which caulk to buy
for leaky drain pipes, how to seal
the basement walls against the winter mold.
At first when she claimed to be a witch,
I knew I couldn't keep her on,

vowed to replace her as soon as I could find
someone else who wasn't prone to casting spells
and had a better grip. But she says
she brings luck to folks she likes,
who take her seriously. Yesterday she gave me
a volume of Keats she got at a yard sale.
So far she's been right about everything.

About Perfection

Behind the wooden counter at Eden Acres Farm-stand,
she scowls over strawberries in flats, discards the overripe,
the green, the blemished or misshapen,

empties them into quart baskets, then lumbers outside
to cull the ears of corn piled high in bins, abandoned
by patrons checking for worms and irregular kernels,
husks pulled down, silk strewn on the ground.

During the lulls, she helps her mother with pies,
blueberry/peach, strawberry/rhubarb, golden-brown
at the edges, carries them from the kitchen in tins,
sets each perfect circle carefully on a pie-stand,
cracked or burnt ones tossed aside.

Frowning at the well-meant banter of customers,
she rings up each transaction in silence,
counts the change without looking up.

And meandering from the bow of her lip to her left nostril,
crooked as the ravine behind the cornfield— a scar.

Affliction

This man prays alone in his pew each Sunday.
A tumor obscures his face,
pendulous, blood-black, so vast

it hides most of what might resemble
human features. And yet he prays.
For what?

For a cure? For forgetfulness?
For a child who would not run away,
a congregant who'd slide in beside him,

look directly into his eyes, extend a hand,
more than a terse greeting, a quick retreat?
And who is listening?

The pious have seen his affliction and turned away,
the stench too fetid, the bloody suffusion too repugnant
to permit human intervention.

He lifts his eyes to the Stations of the Cross,
fourteen stained-glass windows suffused in light,
gazes at stones splashed garnet along the tortured path.

Grasping the back of the polished wooden bench before him,
he rises, moves his lips to the choral anthem,
Yes, There is a Balm in Gilead.

Armed & Dangerous

After convicted burglar Bucky Runningdeer escaped
and shot the Trooper, news coverage crawled to last place,
the cops embarrassed by lost trails and bogus leads
and a bungled almost-capture in the woods near Fredonia,
the shine on their badges dimmed by signs scrawled on barns,
"We Love you, Bucky," "Keep on Running," but painted over
five months later, when two more cops were killed, a Chevy pick-up stolen,
even the Senecas shuddering when a shadow touched the window
or an unusual rustle disturbed the summer night. Yesterday
fourteen Troopers ambushed Bucky in a field near his shack,
weapons cocked on all sides, helicopter flying low over his shoulder
forcing him face down in the brush, his mouth filling with weeds,
arms flung over his head, so tired. Folks cheered. The police waved
as they carted him off, stripped of his hero's welcome, eyes closed,
face set like flint, a blade of grass still clinging to his tongue.

The Hat
Moby Dick, Chapter 130

Beneath the luminescence—
a turgid black sea—
pale form of the leviathan rising,
overlord of the underworld
flaunting his blow-hole
before an arc of blood-
tempered harpoons,
which bend and corrode
between his white ribs,
dragging ropes of hemp
uncoiling fast behind him,
taut in turbulence.

Oh, how the despot rages,
pinioned to the listing deck,
peg-leg trapped in a hole
between heaven and hell,
clinging to a spar which sways
like a compass needle,
head jerking angrily skyward
as he watches a red-billed sea hawk
scream and wheel
in encroaching eddies, dart in
to pluck his prized captain's hat,
dangle it into the distance,
a tiny black spot
tumbling into the depths.

Nelson Mandela Tells a Story

When asked about the important lessons
he had learned in life, Nelson Mandela
tells how he once took his 4-year old grandson
to a shopping mall, the boy clinging to his left hand,
chattering and laughing,

while his grandfather shook the hands of admirers—
his worshipers, people of all races—
Mandela beaming all the while at their adulation
as crowds thrilled to his presence.

Suddenly he felt the child's grasp loosen,
felt him move from his left to his right side,
his face looking directly into Mandela's
as he reached up to recapture
the hand that had stolen his grandfather.

Gluttony

I knew a pig named Louisa,
four hundred pounds of snorting,
rooting bristly hide and slobber,
beloved by crazy Angela

who collared and belled her,
filled her trough with brinjal curry
and pappadams, let her graze
on nasturtiums for dessert.

Louisa's dish was always full
but she felt empty,
pale-lashed eyes forever searching
for delights forbidden.

Once after lunch al fresco, her belly
bloated yet growling with entitlement,
Louisa snuck her speckled snout
alongside Angela's plate of vindaloo,

snaked out her dappled tongue
and sucked it clean, washed it down
with a swig of apple cider
from the tumbler in Angela's hand.

Banished, she waddled from the garden,
falling to her knees beneath the trees
consumed by disappointment,
wanting more.

O Lou. First the appetite,
then the indulgence.
The hunger endures.

IV
...scouting the distance

Anthem
(Psalm 118:24)

This day,
this glittering, overflowing day,
holds me in its architecture,
the textures of its hours,
rooms bursting with bric-a-brac,
living portraits, woven landscapes
humming with sound waves.
Each step along its hallways,
each minute echoes
the tolling of its decay, the measure
of fullness in slow dissolve.

Yet how insistent is the light
that streams through windows, casting
indelible lattice patterns on the carpet,
how enticing, the shadows tilting
from the angle of the door frame,
pouring secrets into the cup of my ear.
The watercolor garden I planted yesterday
blurs behind me in the distance. I live
between the gold-pink streak of rising
and the mauve smoke of resting.
This day is my home.
And I'm glad in it.

Mockingbird

Under a bronze Buddha's eye, too many
cellphone-talkers, crowds at the koi pond.
As I hurry from the Botanical Gardens,

I'm stunned by the song of a plump grey bird
perched on a palm branch, trilling
a nigun like a cantorial soloist.

Catching his bead of eye,
I whistle an improvisation into the air
changing pitch and rhythm with each phrase.
And bubbling from his feathery throat,

a stream of my own fragmented song,
a cantillation winding itself into my ear,
my tune becoming beautiful
because he heard and answered it.

Returning
Rosh Hashanah 2018

A woodsy smell, a familiar light—
home-coming restores wholeness,
the self reunited with the messy residue of history,
treasured pottery cracked but unbroken,
a seasoned skillet, Old Spice hidden in the cabinet.

Once again, September yellow jackets
hum lazily in the hydrangea outside the window.
A letter from a lost friend languishes in the mailbox,
remembrance of a forgotten decade.
Flattened on the bedside table,
an unfinished novel waits to be re-shelved.

This is the New Year, season of returning
to thinning foliage, paled flower beds.
Time to reduce wardrobes to the essentials,
purge pantries of outdated tins, fix leaky pipes.
Time to heal the sunburn, clear away
the detritus of summer holidays,
to collect old promises, honor them.

And pause for a moment
to recapture the dead,
re-discover the living.

Scouting the Distance
for Will and Matt

Two small boys swing
on the frosted wings of angels,
shout riddles across December graves
freshly dug and crusted over,
streak wild through the Memory Garden,
Vale of Tranquility, past the Blue Sky Mausoleum,
mittened fingers machine-gunning between fenceposts
toward Red Jacket's bronze horse
and the Hamilton family obelisk.

They clamber up the slope
to Grandfather's shiny black stone,
cold granite warmed by flushed reflections
as hands trace the familiar letters of their name—
craggy N, two-headed snake of S—
that peers behind itself into the grass
while scouting the distance ahead.

Whooping downhill to Mirror Lake,
its frozen shoreline strewn
with feathers and hard green turds,
they squawk back at teal-headed mallards,
angry white swans with necks extended,
never mind the stink, or frieze
of ice-fractured limbs against the sky.
Stopping before an easel at water's edge,
the boys admire faint watercolor waves
rippling across a canvas.
Brush in hand, the artist steps aside.

Apollo at Fifteen
for Will

Hair streaming over fingerboard
this young god bends
to his unamplified guitar,

plinks and strums, riffs barely audible.
Shifting harmonies float
on waves of improvised sound,

words unformed in his mouth,
his lips following the meanderings
of his fingers across the strings.

Silent for a moment,
he props his downy cheek
against his palm,

searching the horizon
for prophetic almost-songs
of what might be coming

toward him, imagines
his own voice spinning
boldly across the morning sky.

American Girls

For her eighth birthday, she wants doll's clothes.

She'll dress her American Girls
in tea-dresses and bridal gowns;
no grey flannel suits for *her* Girls,
no tiny laptops from the catalogue
to accompany them through the glass ceiling.
What she loves are fabrics, soft and alluring,
tiny gold heels, wants her Amelia, her Maggie
to be adorned in burgundy velvet,
white satin, shimmering with sequins.

Why should she choose the wooly work-week
for the dolls she loves to dress,
when a pair of well-dressed American Guys
might be waiting for them at Mom's house
or in the lobby of Daddy's condo,
to open their doors, lavish gifts upon them,

rescue them from the misfortune
of being pulled apart or abandoned,
hair combed thin, plastic arms extended,
one eyelid stuck half-closed.
With any luck, they'll arrive at the ball
well before midnight on a prince's arm,
shining in the spotlight, chosen.

Coming of Age

She leans against the porch rail,
slender Mountain Ash
demure as a spring debutante
carrying white lace bouquets
for her coming out,

leaves smelling of marzipan
alluring to shy admirers—
neighborhood bees and moths.
But by late August, she's outgrown
her chaste adolescence,

this cousin of the rose family,
more tantalizing than the most
fragrant of her gentle species,
nosegays ripened
into pendant red-orange berries,

bitter but dazzling clusters
more flamboyant than juniper.
She twirls in the autumn wind,
crimson beads exposed
behind a pinnate fringe,

and come November, shows off
her jewels to the winter-poor,
flaunts them shriveled
from brittle limbs, even after
the last leaf has disappeared,

as she intoxicates flocks
of unwary songbirds
with fermented sweetness,
every raucous waxwing
drunk with desire.

November
for Tom on his 40th birthday

Hours before you were born,
I climbed a rickety wooden ladder
propped inside the unfinished frame
of my house-to-be,

to a second story window
where brooms of oak trees
swept clouds from a perfect blue sky,
and clusters of copper coins
shimmered in sun,
stirring in the air like wind chimes,
stubborn leaves of autumn.

Now a mother's wish—
the gift of becoming.
From the wrap-around-porch
of your new house in the woods,
may you watch winter's unspent leaves
turn to brown leather like scraps
of old book bindings worn soft,

and luminous autumns merge
with April mornings, when oaks awake
and slip into their green sleeves,
warmed by dreams of copper
shining against a blue November sky.

Changes
for Elvis

When the dog died something changed.
They said it was time, he was old,
slept a lot and soiled the carpet,

but they felt the absence—
the snuffling, nuzzling,
the heat, the silent approval.

He's better off, they reasoned,
went about re-shuffling their lives,
gratefully sleeping-in.

But when they looked out the window
at the leafless trees beyond his grave,
they noticed for the first time

a boney angularity suddenly exposed,
shadows, once abundant,
vanished in the harsh winter light.

Closing the blinds.
they re-arranged the furniture,
reached for a blanket, each other.

Genesis
homage to Helen Frankenthaler

At the command of the artist's
thumb, elbow, knuckle,
paint soaks into an untreated canvas,
fades opaque to transparent,
watery stains find new paths,
leach into each other, change
direction, collision and innuendo
at every turn, fuzziness at the edges,
crevices bleeding through—
planned imperfections.

Look. A liquid landscape,
a sunset, sweep of anemones—
flat abstractions awash in color fields,
texture of hidden layers
insinuating just below the surface.
Like waves, they morph
beneath a restless ocean,
engulf the shoreline,
ebbing to gather strength,
starting over.

The Bathing Suit

My honeymoon photos
show a slim-hipped, lithe woman
in a printed bikini, bathing cap in hand,
emerging like Venus from the Caribbean,
sun-kissed face smiling confidently,
strolling across the hot sand
toward an adoring husband.

This morning the Florida heat
is reason enough to yank on my
new Land's End purple bathing suit
over the hemispheres of my hips,
its underwire bra barely containing
a cleavage more concave than voluptuous.

But the water is cool and I swim
two lengths of the pool without stopping.
As I race for the cover of my towel,
not one pair of sun-glassed eyes
is raised in judgment from its cell-phone.
And I feel, well, something like svelte…
and possibly divine.

In Praise of Geometry
for Mary Jane

She gave me her photo of a Danish castle,
moat right-angled to rampart wall,
sky reflected on a trapezoid of water.
She chose to capture this particular corner,

painted the waterline an iridescent green,
the sky mottled silver, raked the stone
with rust and mossy cracks, warming
the stark architecture with her artist's eye.

And shining through the wash of color—
an immutable system holding up this world
of ever-changing light and wind, gardens and oceans,
branches shifting against the window,

reminding me there can be no undulating waves,
no birds-in-flight, no sunrise without a horizon,
how the grace of a ballet dancer
depends on a vertical, a plane,

and Cezanne's gauzy foliage loosens itself
over the symmetry and curvature
of a landscape's sturdy shoulders.

I placed the picture in my bedroom
next to a window overlooking the garden,
where I watch vines of pink clematis
twine around a wooden trellis.

Honeycrisp

Let's praise whoever invented
the Honeycrisp apple, a hero in my book,
which includes similar admiration
for the first farmer to turn milk into cheese,
and the Dutchman who whisked-up
the original Hollandaise.

Hooray for the horticulturist
who managed to save
this sterile species from extinction,
rewarding the taste buds of the world
with the juiciness inherent
in its larger than usual cells,
the exquisite toothy-ness of the bite,
the sweetness of concentrated sugars,
far more agreeable than Granny Smith.

Thanks to you, whoever you are,
for giving us Honeycrisp,
wrapped in pink, dappled with rose and yellow,
the only fruit I know where just one taste
is plenty good enough to replace
a brownie or chocolate chip cookie,
and guaranteed to keep the doctor away.

Flag
November, 2016

At Francis Parker #23 School
we began each day with the Pledge,
placing our hands across our sweaters,
intoning "liberty and justice for all,"
comforted that even during
that terrible war "over there,"
we were safe under the flag.

Now our nation's led by a demagogue,
the worst possible instincts unleashed,
insidious fear of "the other"
once seen only in foreign lands
soiling the fabric of our flag,
violence tearing at the selvage edges,
unraveling the stripes, the stars.

My generation knows what's lost,
and although tested through the decades
by the inequities of our imperfect union,
we remain naïve as school-children
believing someday we'll reclaim
this embattled homeland,
lifting our faces each morning to find
something like hope billowing overhead.

We Never Close

How comforting it is to whiz past
the convenience store whose neon sign
proclaims to anyone interested enough to look
that there will always be a welcome place
at the corner of Forest and Elmwood,

that an eternal light glows inside,
illuminating more than one angel
with arms outstretched,
who would pull up a chair
and listen to your story.

At night the blue letter "C" flickers and fades,
leaving a ghostly promise,
"WE NEVER LOSE,"
that folks can shuffle in at any hour
to find the minutes they wasted waffling
or buy back lost chances,

that elderly couples might regain
years spent in quibble and bicker,
mourners redeem unused caresses,
if only a wind-tossed passer-by
would push the grimy handle
he'd be uplifted in a rush of yes.

But few dare to navigate the shoals
of tossed condoms, wrappers in the doorway,
or risk finding only lottery tickets
and dusty tabloids inside,
and a clerk shifting wearily on aching feet.

The faithful race by, heads bowed,
reassured that a sanctuary
might be available at this corner at any hour,
if ever they should need one.

About the Author

Born in Rochester, NY, Susan Dworski Nusbaum received her BA from Smith College and her law degree from the University of Buffalo Law School. She lives in Buffalo NY where she has worked as a musician, teacher, arts administrator, and most recently as a criminal prosecutor. Her poetry collection, "What We Take With Us," released by Coffeetown Press in 2014, was a finalist in the Brittingham/Pollack Prize Competition. Her second poetry collection, "Open Wide, the Eye," was released June 1, 2016. (Coffeetown Press)

Her work has appeared in numerous publications including The Connecticut Review, Poetry East, Nimrod International Journal, Chautauqua Literary Journal, Chautauqua, Harpur Palate, Woven Tale Press, Calliope (June 2020), Wisconsin Review, The Sow's Ear, Earth's Daughters, The Buffalo News, and A Celebration of Western New York Poets, (2014).

A participant in the Chautauqua Institution Writers' Festivals and Chautauqua Writers' Center poetry workshops, Susan served on the Board of the Chautauqua Literary Arts Friends. She has presented her work in solo public readings in numerous communities, including Buffalo NY, Rochester NY, Washington DC, Chautauqua NY, and Sarasota FL.

www.ingramcontent.com/pod-product-compliance
Lightning Source LLC
Chambersburg PA
CBHW011407070526
44586CB00022B/2591